Born to Tell

Jennifer Lewis

AuthorHouse™
1663 Liberty Drive
Bloomington, IN 47403
www.authorhouse.com
Phone: 1-800-839-8640

All the names and characteristics of the persons included in this book, living or dead, have been changed or are purely coincidental.

First published by AuthorHouse 9/2/2011

ISBN: 978-1-4634-4495-2 (e)
ISBN: 978-1-4634-4497-6 (sc)

Library of Congress Control Number: 2011913629

Printed in the United States of America

This book is printed on acid-free paper.

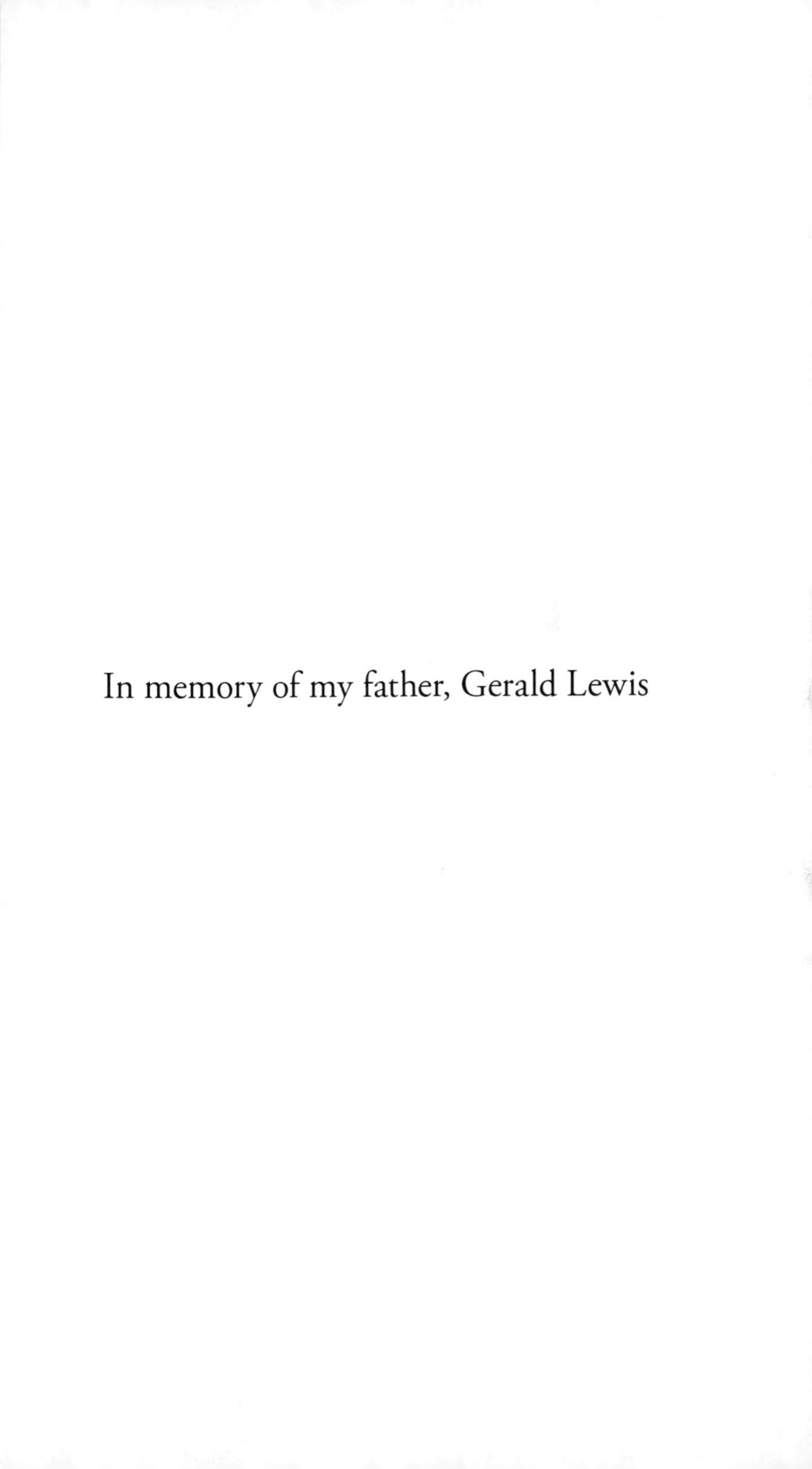

In memory of my father, Gerald Lewis

Acknowledgments

I would like to thank everyone who helped me in realizing the dream of writing this book. Thanks to Kal, Elaine, Guy, Dorothy, and Heather and to my son David for their support, patience, and encouragement throughout the endeavor. I would like to offer a special thank you to all my teachers who made me who I am. Most of all I would like to thank everyone who never judged me but gave me a chance.

This is a test of faith, love and affection, and proof that the heart can heal on its own through forgiveness. The sickness that festers in some lives boils like anger and is ready to erupt, damaging the souls, hearts, minds, and lives of everyone affected. To gain control of my life, to live the life I was born to live to the fullest, I had to heal my broken heart. I had to forgive the unforgivable and learn how to live all over again.

It is a miracle I survived to tell my story about the duppies and the obeah and the horrible beatings and threats of what would happen to me if I did not do what I was told to do even when I knew it was not right.

Living with the duppies and the obeah and the beatings was like living in hell. I had to endure pain while I pretended to the world that all was great when I was dying inside.

Those were not beatings. I remember calling them "murderations," because the blows were so deadly and I felt like I was not going to make it through the episode. Once I was beaten so badly that I had what felt like an out-of-body experience. It was as if I was watching someone else getting the beating and not me. I had stopped feeling the blows.

From generation to generation, beatings were all our parents knew. That was their idea of how to discipline us and help us grow, thereby carving us into their perception of what they considered good and acceptable to society. That perception continues to ruin lives and scars our bodies and our minds.

The beatings involved belts, tree limbs, ropes made from tree vines, electric wires, hoses, stones, and whatever could be found to use as a weapon to inflict pain on us. The beatings were what Mother knew best; she had endured and survived them too.

Once she did the unthinkable during a rage. I was crying and watching my sister Julie undergoing a horrible murderation one night when there was nothing I could do to prevent it.

When it was supposed to be over, after what seemed like hours of physical abuse and did not seem satisfying enough for her punishment, Mother did something almost unconceivable. She pulled her ratchet knife and opened it and slashed my sister, who was trying to shelter the blows by hiding under the table. Mother got her straight in the face with her knife right under the table.

There was blood everywhere. I was terrified and screaming like crazy. Mother was foaming at the mouth, the spitting image of the devil.

She asked me if I wanted some too, if I wouldn't shut up. I was shaking because of what I had just witnessed. Of course I didn't want some too! I wanted someone to come and rescue me and to save us. I wanted her to send me to Germany to the couple Mother had heard was looking for a little girl to adopt. I was hanging on to that hope. It was all I had.

She kicked my sister Julie out of the house that night, bleeding. I could not sleep all night. I could hear Julie under the cellar all night. I knew she needed medical attention, but I was so scared and could not do anything to help her. I had to protect myself first by staying quiet and invisible and cautious in the one room so as not to get Mother's frustrations any higher so that she might turn on me.

I was also terrified of the rats, spiders, scorpions, and other creepy crawlers that lived under that dark and cold cellar, and especially afraid of the ghosts lurking around our house;

Julie had to be outside with them and injured. I did not realize that that night was to prepare me for a future of how much more heartless my siblings would become.

As daylight came, I was the first one to go outside to check on my sister. Everyone else carried on with their normal lives as if nothing had happened. My sister Paula was not moved by what had happened to Julie.

In fact she was quite pleased and walked around with a chip on her shoulder and felt that Julie had deserved the chop in her face and the beating because Julie had stolen her school fees and then spent some of the money to buy food for herself and her friends.

I was deeply affected by my family's insensitivity and the insanity and was in a daze. I wondered what would become of me and if I would survive to become an adult.

The dog had just had its puppies in an old empty barrel that was lying underneath the squalid cellar. Julie had removed the dog and its puppies from the barrel and taken refuge in it; that's where she had spent the night.

The worst part is that after the beatings, you did not dare to tell anyone about them or the injuries that resulted from them. You'd go to school the next day and think of a good lie to tell your teacher or anyone who asked you about them, because we were warned that if we ever told anyone that our parents or guardians had harmed us, the consequences would be dire.

Sometimes the explanation we gave for the cuts and bruises were bizarre and did not explain our injuries. It was common to see a student in class looking like he or she had had a rough night. It made me feel like I was not alone and that it was normal and not in my family alone.

It was the silent norm for parents to beat their children mercilessly, and it was not talked about. Otherwise it could create huge conflicts between the parent and anyone else who got involved. It could sometimes become deadly if a neighbor interfered with a parent who was disciplining his or her child. Most times injuries got covered up and healed externally. Internally we were scarred for life.

The heart learns to deal with the pain of the past. We shared our secrets only with our closest friends who were also going through the same thing in their homes.

Sometimes we would see our friends in the mornings, and we were all pitchy patchy. Sometimes all that was left for us to do was compare our bruises and wipe our tears away.

I always knew if I was going to get a beating in the night or if it would be someone else in my house. Sometimes we would sell each other out to save our own skin. Even now that we are adults, resentments still have a hold on us and we remain divided as we grow from the pains of the past.

On the night of a beating, Mother always slept with the hose or stick or the electric wire or the tamarind whip or whatever she planned to use in her pillowcase or on the floor underneath the bed beside the chimmy (chamber pot). There was no escaping a beating if you were promised one. There was nowhere to go and nowhere to run to.

Mother, my siblings and I lived in a one-room house with one exit and outdoor facilities. At night we would have to bring in the white enamel chimmy and place it under the bed so we could use it during the night. It was advisable never to go outside at nights or you could get hit by a duppy (ghost) that could leave you dumb or deaf or very sick. Your family would be unable to find a cure for you.

Getting hit by a duppy could cause you

sudden and unexplainable sicknesses, paralysis, and even death. The doctors thought a girl I knew had cerebral palsy, but her family obeah man insisted that she was possessed with evil spirits because her mother was hit by a duppy while she was pregnant. Her middle-class family became poverty stricken after spending their entire earnings and lost properties on obeah men and obeah women whom they hoped would heal their daughter. She was never healed.

It was my job to take out the chimmy every morning and empty it and clean it and get it ready for the next night. If I forgot to bring the chimmy in, I would be awakened and told to go outside and get it. At that age, it felt like the worst job on the planet, but I had no other choice. I had to do it willingly for fear of being beaten. I always felt that it was a chore that should be shared and not left to one individual since all of us were emptying our bladders in the same piss pot at nights.

My mother and I and my sisters Julie and Paula shared the same bed. Mother was not fair to Julie, who had to wash the sheets every morning before school even if it had not been her who had wet the bed during the night.

Madonna, my eldest sister, was back from preaching the word of God all over the Caribbean Islands and was pregnant by the gardener at the church she was stationed at in Mobay (Montego Bay). While visiting on vacation I would watch my sister band her pregnant belly before going into the church and pulpit to preach and clap and sing like a bird to the congregation who did not know what she was hiding. I knew the secret was not right, but I had to keep quiet for fear I would be beaten or snuffed out. I wondered what God was thinking, and I would hide my face.

As time went by, Madonna's belly became noticeable and she had to resign. The church could not have an unmarried pregnant woman preaching from its pulpit. Madonna had to come home with a baby from the Rastafarian man who did not want to marry her. That was the end of her preaching career and the beginning of the cycle of single parenthood in our family.

Rock is my elder brother and was permanently given away in the country to a woman named Miss Veggie and her husband, Mass Vintent, who lived deep in the cockpits of Jamaica. One day Mother brought me to the country to meet Rock for the first time. I remembered how scary, high, narrow, and slippery the mountainside was with the precipice below leading up to the board house on the pinnacle of the mountain through the bushes.

Mother said that the couple had wanted

a baby but had fertility problems. They were "as poor as church mice" and could offer only a life of hard work in the fields for his food. Mother insisted that whenever she gave us away it was for the best.

Most nights we could not sleep because it was someone's turn to get a beating from Mother. Rock and Owen, my eldest brother, and my eldest sister, Madonna, had escaped some of that madness when they were shipped off.

Jules, Paula, and I would be up for hours and unable to sleep, even though we might have school in the morning. The thought of going to get a beating in the night made it difficult to fall asleep.

My mother would beat us just after we fell asleep, or if she dozed off before us, it would be in the wee hours of the morning just before daybreak, when we were finally sleeping deeply. We would be awakened by the blows on our skin.

Everyone would be awakened from the screams and the frenzy of whoever was getting the lashes. With sleep in our eyes and almost overpowering us, we cowered in the corners of the room, fearful we would get hit accidentally because the room was so small.

For years I was terrified of falling asleep. Even when I became an adult and was living on my own, I was haunted by the memories of being beaten during the night. Many nights I awoke from nightmares with my hands in the air to defend myself from my mother's lashes only to find out that I was just having another nightmare. The beatings were the last thing I thought about before I fell asleep at nights.

I was born in Allman Town, Regent Street, Kingston, Jamaica, in 1967, about a block from National Heroes Circle, where my favorite national hero and founder of the Jamaica

Labor Party, Sir Alexander Bustamante, is buried. Busta, as he was affectionately called, was also the first prime minister of Jamaica after we gained independence in 1962.

I was very fortunate to have attended his funeral by accident. I was running away from my grandmother's home that day because Fayette, my cousin, had given me a beating for not wanting to go back to the shop after I had already been there ten times for one meal.

I soon realized that the bus was not running and the streets were blocked. I was caught up in the crowd and the excitement and celebration of the day of Sir Alexander Bustamante's funeral. At the end of the day I had to return home to Fayette, who grabbed my ears and almost wrung them off, causing them to hurt me for several days.

Mr. Gerald Lewis, the man with the donkeys and cart who delivered ice throughout the community seven days a week and who had

had a drink with every man in the community, was my father, and I loved him with all my heart.

I was nearly five years old when my mother decided to leave my father and steal us away one day when he was at work. I remember the day when a big truck came to the house. I did not want to go. Even at that young age I knew something was terribly wrong.

I wanted Papa to come home and catch them, but he did not. I still imagine the heartache and the devastation he must have felt when he came home to an empty house—no wife, no kids, no furniture—and his future destroyed.

I had objected to the conspiracy to leave my father in such a heartless manner, especially after my mother had proclaimed how much he had helped her and Madonna and given them a break to live in the city. He had enabled Mother to escape her father's brutal regime.

Her own father had stopped her from going to school and made her work in the fields because he claimed she was now able to read.

Having had seven children (two passed away at childbirth), she met my father. She said in those days that when a woman was ready to have her baby, she usually prepared the room and delivered the baby by herself.

She said that a woman would be lucky to have a midwife present if one was living nearby. She said that two of my siblings did not survive childbirth because she tried to deliver them herself.

The first time my mother visited Kingston, some friends who lived in the capital introduced her to my father as a possible prospect. My father fell in love with her, but she saw him only as an opportunity. She accepted his commitment, a life and future together, but did so without a hint of love or sincerity.

According to my mother he was perfect for

her because he had his own place, he was well known in the community, and he had a job. All she had to do was to move in.

She got rid of my brothers Owen and Rock and kept Madonna and moved into my father's house. Paula and Julie were born a few years later.

After being with my father for almost fifteen years, my mother decided to stage an elaborate wedding and spend everything my father had saved. Two years later I was born of this "special" love.

Julie always called me "Daddy's girl." She was envious, so the one thing that made me feel good about myself also made me feel bad. Julie taunted me every step of the way in my life.

I grew distant from my siblings and was never given a chance to bond with them. None of them ever said to me, "Honey, you made a mistake." It was always a bitch lick from them, a slap or a blow that sometimes made me see stars. I was never hugged or told I was loved by my mother until I was nearly thirty years old. It wasn't that she did not want to; it was because she did not know how to.

It was not until I became an adult and realized that I had not received the love I deserved that I made a point of giving myself the love I never had. I also reached out to my friends to obtain the love and affection missing in my life so I would never be alone again. In the meantime, my siblings became carbon copies of my mother.

After the truck drove off, our lives were never the same. The resentment toward each other grew, preventing healing as my mother and my sibling's hearts turned into stone. There was nothing my father could do or say to make them forgive him for what they claimed he did.

My father suffered depression and spiraled

into an even deeper depression because of what my mother had done to him. He had to be hospitalized. In spite of his efforts to make peace with his wife and family, he died with a broken heart.

When my mother heard the news that he had died, her reaction was, "He should have been dead a long time ago." Her callousness hurt me more than his actual passing, and I will never know what he had to be sorry for, since he was the one who did what was good. He was the one whose heart was broken.

My mother got what she came to Kingston for—a better life and a new start. That was all she wanted. Now she and my siblings could make it on their own. My father became dispensable and suddenly acquired faults. Ungrateful, they forgot where they had come from and chose to use and hurt the only man who cared for them.

My mother claimed to have fallen out

of love with my father. She began to dislike everything about him: his walk, the way he talked, even the way he chewed his food. She began to plan how she would take us away to spite him. She had already started to build a new life herself and had moved her own mother the sixty-six miles from Trelawny to a few houses away from us in Kingston.

She also reclaimed Owen from the people in the country he had been given to. He was to live with her mother and her sister's two abandoned children, Fayette and Tommy, whose mother went to England when they were babies and had other children and never looked back at these two children until they were adults. My mother had raised her sister's two children with hatred and resentment toward them. Her sister had left them behind when mother had her own children to provide for and to worry about.

Madonna my eldest sister became free of

me when the plan to leave my father came into action. Mother made her join the Salvation Army. All my life Madonna has said I was a burden to her. She never lets me forget how our mother turned her into a woman before her time, forcing me on her so she had to take care of me when I was a baby.

She never lets me forget how she used to have to journey through Race Course (National Heroes Park) in the blazing hot sun to take me to day care before and after school every day. She lets me know how I was big and fat and could not walk too far.

She lets me know how often she was late for school because of me and had to carry this big baby on her side that was not hers. To this day Madonna still resents me for robbing her of her childhood.

I can't seem to apologize enough for my mother's mistakes. They affected not only Mother; they ruined her family relationships and also made her children unable to give or to receive unconditional love and affection from each other.

I suffered a lot because my mother was almost never around, and when she was it was just to beat us. I only saw her a few waking hours each day when she was in commando mode. I realized early on in life that I was better off without her, but I chose to honor my mother, as God tells us we should.

I thought Madonna was my mother for a long time, because my mother worked a lot. Many days I was left with the security guard because day care had closed and no one came to pick me up. Madonna claims that she had detention for late arrival at school in the morning.

I know from the way she was dirty that she had had a good game of dandy-shandy (a famous outdoor ballgame enjoyed by both sexes in Jamaica) with her friends and had forgotten about me again. Her job was getting difficult, and she could no longer pull her weight.

Mother decided that Madonna would be better off with the Salvation Army at that point, so she sent her to live there. This also ended the journey to the Catholic Church with Madonna, a place where poor people went to get food and clothes a few times a year.

We would wait in the boiling-hot sun in the line all day. Sometimes we'd get so many bags of food we'd have enough to share with strangers. At the end of the day when we got home we'd often find that they were filled with weevils and worms.

We would sieve out anything that moved from the flour and the cornmeal. We would remove the lumps from the sugar and powdered milk. If not moving with crawlers it was usually rock hard and had to be pounded to be powdery again as it was the only source of milk in our house. Even today I still hear the sound of biting gravel in the bulgur and the rice.

Suddenly, Madonna was physically out of our lives. My life then became harder than I thought. I ended up living with my grandmother a few doors from my father's house, but he was not allowed to see me. My sisters and my mother were staying with a friend, where my father would not be able to find them.

My cousin Fayette who lived in the house with grandmother, my brother Owen and Tommy who lived under the cellar because he had had idle hands, made sure she enforced my mother's rule that I was not to see my father and that my father was not to see me. I was ushered inside the home whenever my father was passing by our yard. Because of my mother's selfishness, and without any explanation, I was separated from my father, whom I loved dearly.

While living at my grandmother's house I learned that eating bread dipped in water curbed the hunger. There was no kitchen or cupboard or box with any food anywhere, so you learned to eat whatever was given to you. Whenever there was food in that house, it was eaten immediately.

There was never enough of anything but rats and roaches. The bedbugs were worse than the ants, and the scorpions hid in our clothes. We had no electricity, and I had never seen a television set then.

My grandmother Humaa used the little battery radio only to listen to BBC in the mornings. If the battery was weak and there was no money to replace it for weeks, she would take the batteries out of the radio in the morning and place them in the sunlight to charge them; then she would replace them and we would get just enough power to listen the news as it slowly died again.

Humaa (for grandmother) was a Maroon descendant from Maroon Town. Her parents' parents' parents were brought to Jamaica from Africa during the slave trade and had become runaway slaves of Maroon Town who hid in the mountains. Later they became freed slaves. Besides telling me their favorite duppy stories, grandmother always told me to pay attention to the man in the moon, who appears to be carrying a bundle of wood on his head, signifying that the purpose of man's life on earth is to work. I took that wisdom with me on my journey through life.

Fayette's brother Tommy was in his early teens. He had problems with his fingers; he was a thief. People referred to him as the one who was able to steal milk from the cup of coffee in front of you without you knowing. He was such a kleptomaniac that he was not allowed to come inside the board house we shared with Humaa, Owen, and Fayette. Tommy, with his few pieces of clothes and a torn-out cardboard box for his bed, lived under the squalid cellar of our little box of a room that stood on four posts exposed to the mercy of the world and the elements.

If only his mother knew the life of hell and turmoil her son lived, filled with resentment and abandonment from his own family, whom she entrusted with his care. A life without love and no hope for the future was what my mother gave him and his sister. Life took a bitter turn for all of us still. It became more about surviving than living.

My grandmother, who seemed to be the only one who wanted me, was now sick and could no longer walk. We could not go to the corner store together, which she liked doing. I now went on my own while she waited by the doorway a few feet from her bed until I returned. Humaa deteriorated so fast; I did not know what caused the sudden change in her health.

Even though I was a little girl, I knew my grandmother needed me for more than to help her put her okra slime into her eyes for her glaucoma, but because Fayette was so hard on her and she could no longer look after herself, she needed me to help her.

I took on the job of her caregiver, with my sixty-pound body lifting my two-hundred-pound grandmother onto the bucket for as many times as she needed to go during the day. Fayette was very rough with my grandmother, and you could feel grandmother's fear of her. Grandmother was very unhappy. I took care of her as best as I could until Mother took me away from her again.

As for Tommy, besides my father, he was the second most disliked male in my family. They treated him worse than anyone I knew other than my father. Sometimes it was sickening to watch how they treated their own family.

Even when he cried out for help, his cries landed on deaf ears. He soon wandered away from us from under the cellar to start his own life. I did not see him again until my grandmother was near death and he came to make amends with her.

My grandmother kept her thread bag (a purse made from cloth with a string) in her bosom to protect what little money she had safe from idle hands that did no other work but steal. I lived at my grandmother's house until one day my mother came to visit us and told us she had found a place and that I and my sisters would be reuniting. My mother had found a room to rent in Havendale, and that was the first time I went to school.

My mother had taken up going to Pocomania churches and working obeah. Pocomania churches were backyard churches that included spiritual readings (psychic readings). The pastor of such churches is always the obeah man or obeah woman who does acts and claims to be able to free you from bad spirits or ghosts, as they are also called. Obeah is a curse you cast on someone you don't like. No one is ever proud to say that he or she is involved in obeah, because it is always conducted in secret and frowned upon.

My mother's first obeah woman was Sister Vie. My mother became one of her best customers. The two became such close friends that my mother moved us a few doors away from her, and Sister Vie became our doctor. Mother had me attending a school close by our yard while Paula and Julie were still attending Allman Town Primary. After school I would stay at the obeah woman's house until my mother came from work at nights to pick me up.

I took lunch to school every day, but I was

not well adjusted, so I could not eat my lunch. I would bring my lunch home and eat it in the night just before Mother came to pick me up from Sister Vie's house.

One day a boy from that house decided to take my lunchbox. I refused to give it to him, and he pushed me through a glass door, six steps down, and out the door. I was barely sixty pounds, and I bled like a slaughtered animal.

My arm was chopped open in two different places. They brought a white enamel basin to catch the blood. They washed it and iced it and put on a mixture of nutmeg dressing and did everything they could to stop the bleeding until my mother came home. I was in pain and was suffering. I prayed that my mother would come and take me to the doctor.

She finally arrived and listened to their version of the incident. I thought I would be taken to a doctor, but I was not. My mother decided that my arm was no longer bleeding and that I would be fine. So I was given more bandages, a sling was made for my arm, and the obeah woman provided some more dressing.

School was short-lived, as Mother decided to move us to Trenchtown (where Bob Marley grew up). My father was still missing from my life, and every thought about what they did to him hurt my tiny heart as each day passed. I ached for my grandmother, but being able to help her was beyond my control. I was now merely trying to survive in Trenchtown myself.

We lived on Tobias Street next to the gully that runs through Jungle and Trenchtown. The gunshots were like music to your ears, and soon we didn't run anymore. Trenchtown is still one of the worst places to live in Kingston. It was also the place with the biggest tenement yard we ever lived in. The four bathrooms and four toilets were built in rows like a courtyard setting and accommodated the nearly hundred people and their guests who used them each day.

One day, something magical happened. A tenant named Miss Hermine, the fisherman's woman, bought a thirteen-inch black-and-white television set. I was six years old, and it was the first time I had seen a television set. I was amazed and wondered if anyone knew whether the people were actually *in* the box.

Miss Hermine and her husband could no longer go to bed early because up to sixty or seventy people would be up watching that one thirteen-inch black-and-white television set late into the night. The nights when *Dracula* and *Dark Shadows* were on were the most crowded. People would bring their own chairs and munchies, and we would watch movies till dawn in the open night air, providing there was no rain.

My mother was still the biggest hypocrite

I've ever known. She was friendly to everyone and their children during the movies. After the movies we would go back to our rooms and she would warn us that whenever she was at work we should stay indoors. We were not to go outside and play with the neighbors' kids; we were to keep to ourselves.

That was one rule that we were never able to follow that well. Sometimes we decided to accept the beating, which was not equivalent to the few minutes we played with our friends. Sometimes we would keep watch for each other so that Mother would not catch us outside or our friends inside. Sometimes the watcher forgot to watch, warranting a triple beating for the night. Sometimes we prayed that she would be tired and her strength would be diminished by the time she got to us.

We had learned that the previous tenant had hanged himself in our room. As a child I was terrified of staying in that room alone and would do anything not to be left alone in it. My mother was even bitterer than everyone thought. You would think that she would know how terrified we were to stay in that room alone and would beat us if we went outside without her permission. You would think that mother would be happier after being separated from my father, but she wasn't.

It was then that I started to experience physical abuse from my mother. It was then that I saw my sisters coming into their evil ways, which they have now perfected. Julie got so many beatings and scars because she would not listen and was more of a tomboy and looked forward to her daily beatings. She would light up when my mother was going to beat me, but I rarely got a beating, because I listened most of the time.

My mother would pretend to befriend the neighbors and their children. It seemed like all was well on the outside, but inside we were threatened. When she went to work we were not to play with the neighbors' children. We were told to stay inside all day with our books. There were no toys except for the ones we made. Nor was there a television or radio in our house, because Mother could not afford those things for us.

That was a hard rule—to not to play with the neighbors' children. The three of us would often conspire to break it after we got bored, fatigued, and hungry and needed some fresh air and exercise from the little tiny room.

If my mom came back suddenly and we got caught outside, my siblings would be prepared for their beating in the night, because it would be difficult for her to catch them. When my mother called me for my beating, I went willingly. I figured I might as well get it over with and not be scared to pass her, because I never knew when she might grab me or throw something at me if I was expecting a beating.

One day my mother decided to visit a lady I had never met before. At the end of the visit, I was told that the lady was my godmother and I would have to stay with her for a while. I did not see or hear from my mother again for months.

There was no phone. A letter from my mother would be out of the question. It must have been out of guilt, but later she picked me up. I was happy that she did not forget me and I could finally come home and go back to school.

My mother had taken up working obeah on my father. She found a married man at the obeah woman's church and was in some sort of relationship with him. She complained to him about many things, including my father, and suddenly out of the blue my father was accused of working obeah on her and her children.

Performing obeah includes dealing with

the dead to cast spells on someone or remove them. Obeah is connected to duppies. Duppies are dead people who did not make it to heaven and can return in the form of a man or an animal with the power to do anything, mostly evil.

Even if I believed there was such a thing as a duppy, my father had no reason to harm his children. I later learned that he was terrified of what we were going through with my mother's rage, as she had already floored him so many times in front of us, and he worried what would become of us.

My poor father had no idea that my mother had gone to an obeah man all our life, claiming to protect us from him and his obeah. That was totally impossible, because when I found my father again, I was twenty-three years old. I was shocked that he still had my mother's wedding picture on his bureau. To my knowledge that was all he had left of her that he cherished. My mother had destroyed all of their wedding pictures in a fire during one of her rages.

My father was an honorable man and was not involved in any iniquity to destroy anyone. My mother's illusion led to her meeting Mr. Barnold, who came into our lives, took our innocence, and distorted what was left of any normal future we may have ever dreamed of.

I soon realized that it was he who introduced my mother to Sister Vie and her spiritualist backyard churches and her obeah-working colleagues and their facilities. This woman would tell my mother that we would not amount to anything and that our father was trying to harm us. She said there was evil sent into our house by our father to kill us.

My poor mother would believe all this jargon and give most of her money to Sister Vie in return for her protection from the evil and for removing ghosts from our house and around the yard. It was never enough.

According to Sister Vie the ghosts were getting stronger, and the hundreds of Psalms given to us to read every morning, noon, and night weren't working. The many pigeon-blood baths the obeah woman required each of us to take, which cost hundreds of dollars, did not keep the evil away.

My mother became addicted to the obeah men and obeah women. Mr. Barnold introduced her to them, proclaiming each one to be better than the other.

My mother became so obsessed with them that even when we were sick she did not take us to a regular doctor anymore but instead took us to the obeah man. Otherwise called a bush-doctor, the obeah man claimed to heal many sicknesses and diseases upon the land. He was always happy to see my mother, as he was mixing up potions for us to drink at a hefty price.

Money was always a problem for my mother, even though she worked most days. Every week one of us would have an appointment with the obeah man, and sometimes two or all of us would end up with appointments on the same day.

Sometimes we would be so exhausted going from one crowded drugstore to the next from Princess Street to Spanish Town Road to fill the obeah man's prescriptions. It was especially crowded on a Saturday morning downtown trying to find the oils and potions the obeah man had ordered us to buy to further protect our house from the duppies.

The obeah pharmacies were packed and hot and sweaty and filled with pickpockets, idlers, peddlers, and looters, but we spent every Saturday morning looking for her drugs. If we were unable to go on Saturday morning because my mother had to work, we would go on Sunday morning bright and early before Pocomania church.

Money was tight, so we had to go to all the stores to see which had the cheaper product. We would buy the cheapest ones and then go to the other stores to buy the obeah oil products and concoctions. For the obeah bush products we had to go to the Coronation Market on Spanish Town Road, where most of the country people from all over the island came to sell their produce.

Some of these country people brought rare bushes not found in the city to sell. Some were tea bushes, such as mint and aloes, for instance, and some were rare bushes and weeds used for boiling and drinking or boiling and then mixing with other deadly bushes and potions to make baths.

Some bushes were hard to find for a particular spell or cure and would sometimes cause for my mother to find another obeah man or obeah woman to get a different prescription.

Coronation Market is one of the worst places to be on a Saturday morning in Jamaica, but it is the only place in Kingston where you can find almost any bush medicine that you want.

It is the busiest marketplace in Jamaica, crowded and filled with moving carts packed with food and running over your feet. If you are not quick enough to get out of the way, you can be seriously injured.

My mother wanted to "kill two birds with one stone," so while she was getting her bush for her medicine, she would also shop for whatever we needed for our home in the market or on the roadside outside the market on Spanish Town Road. There traffic and people moved bumper to butt, butt to bumper.

During the hassle of trying to move through

the crowd with us, Mother was always furious if we were separated from her. Whenever we got caught up to her, she would bring us close to her and bite our ear and tell us to listen to her. Then she would twist our ears so hard it hurt for days.

After the market we made the trip through the crowd with our bags to the bus stop, all the time protecting our valuables from the thieves. We sometimes waited at the bus stop for hours because the buses were so full that we were unable to board.

Sometimes we squeezed in; other times one or two of us would hang off the door of the moving bus. Not until passengers started to arrive at their destination were we able to pile in properly.

We were in no position to tell our mother that we did not want to go with her to the market or that we did not wish to do something she told us to do. That was not an option, and we feared losing a tooth or our hearing. When my mother said, “Jump!” we asked, “How high?”

My mother trusted Mr. Barnold too much. He would take us to lonely beaches without her, under the pretense that he was taking us to teach us how to swim. The lessons and how he held us and where he held us made us realize that these were not just swimming lessons.

One day he tried to touch me inappropriately. When I objected to his touch, he let me go in deep water so I could take in water. I could feel the sand moving beneath my feet. It was as if the sea was taking me in. I felt his arm pull me out from under the water just as I was about to give up on life.

According to him I would obey him next time. Sitting on the shore with my bloated stomach watching my siblings have fun in the water, I planned how this would be my last day going to sea with them.

As the years went by, my mother continued to work obeah to remove the evil spells she claimed were caused by my father. Mr. Barnold continued to introduce us to many different obeah workers.

One in particular, called Mr. Dead, lived high in the mountains. He claimed to possess some power, as after being proclaimed dead he arose at his funeral, knocking from his coffin. My mother took me to the obeah man's home the first time when she thought I was sick. I was having frequent headaches and did not know why. Instead of a physician, she took me to the bush doctor for medicine.

Mother decided that I would take Julie to Mr. Dead, who was just taking her money and boiling potions for us to drink. It is a miracle that we are still alive. She thought his medicines were working and that we were being cured from the ailments he diagnosed. I had no faith in his so-called powers and told myself it was trickery. Surely it wouldn't work for me since I had no faith in the dangerous unproven theories of these potions.

My mother believed that this man's tricks would work to bring us good luck and prosperity. The journey to the mountain to see Mr. Dead was treacherous: a three-hour drive from Kingston on the country bus that was always "packed like sardines in a can" (a proverb). It made a thousand stops before we got to our destination.

After that horrible ride on the bus, we walked what seemed like another ten miles up a steep hill in the boiling sun on a dusty and rocky road. Vehicles rarely made it to the top without great difficulty, and it was just as hard for a man to climb; even mules had trouble climbing that mountain.

Mother sent me and Julie on this journey

with one ripe banana and just enough money to buy one sky juice (ice, syrup, and water) that we were to share on our way back. I was very tired. Mother had already sent me a couple of times that week alone, but she wanted Julie to learn the way as well.

I felt that I was not going to make it that day because the sun was so hot. I was hungry and tired. It was Julie's first time, and she was too anemic to handle the trip. I felt very sorry for her. Julie suggested that we share the banana, but I told her to have it all because I could see that she needed the energy much more than I did to survive that hill.

She insisted on sharing it with me, but I told her I'd take it all if she didn't need it; one of us had to make it back to the city. She decided that she would have it all, and I was happy with that. I was willing to wait a few more hours until we got to Kingston, where we would share the one sky juice between the two of us before our one-hour walk home.

When we finally made it to Mr. Dead's, we waited our turn to pay the money Mom gave us and picked up our weekly Psalms to read for protection. Then we started our journey back down the hill. It had been a burden in the first place, but the burden of leaving and going down the hill seemed much lighter.

When I was running down that hill, tired and hungry and seeing how sick Julie was, I made the decision to never climb that hill again. No matter what my mother said or did to me, that was it, just like the day I decided never to go to sea with them again.

We headed for the bus stop and waited for our bus. It arrived with standing capacity only. We were jam-packed for the three-hour ride back to Kingston.

We got off the bus at Half-Way Tree and decided to buy the sky juice. By this time we were dehydrated, weak, and hungry from the journey in the hot sun. We had money for one juice, which we decided to share to prepare us for our one-hour walk home. We did not have enough money for the bus fare for the second bus home after paying the obeah man.

Most shocking out of this is that many people still take trips to the island to visit their obeah men and continue to waste their money because they believe that the obeah men can help them with their sicknesses and diseases and gives them good luck.

If my mother and others would spend their money on their children instead of on removing ghosts, their children would have a better quality of life. I know how much my mother spent on obeah men instead of us.

The addiction empties their pockets; there is just never enough money. Sometimes one family has more than one obeah man to pay for bewitching or switching or giving bad or good luck. It is a terrible addiction most prevalent in blacks in the Caribbean. I lived and breathed this all my life and hated every moment of it.

As night approached, Mother began to prepare for the duppies. She got the cold stove ready with charcoal. She put the bushes we bought at the market on burning charcoal and sprinkled potions on the fire, making it smoke with a peculiar smell to chase away the duppies. Then she walked around the house clockwise with the smoke-filled burning substance chanting the Twenty-Third Psalm from the Holy Bible: "The Lord is My Shepherd. I shall not want. He leadeth me beside the still waters. He restoreth my soul: he leadeth me in the paths of righteousness for his name's sake. Yea, though I walk through the valley of the shadow of death, I will fear no evil: for thou art with me, thy rod and thy staff they comfort me. Thou preparest a table before me in the presence of my enemies: thou anointest my head with oil; my cup runneth over. Surely goodness and mercy shall follow me all the days of my life: and I will dwell in the house of the Lord forever."

The duppies supposedly dislike this peculiar burning smell in the air and dislike hearing the chanting of the powerful words of God. While hearing the Bible, the duppies lose their power. It is believed that if a duppy comes to harm you, he will return to whoever sends him with more power in his wrath if the sender is not protected.

After supper we would gear up with our Bibles because the readings prescribed for the evening by the obeah man was ready to begin. We spent about two hours every evening reading to protect us when the duppies came.

We read as fast as we could in order to get to the neighbor's room to watch television till bedtime, when the second phase of our readings began before we went to bed. If someone was going to get a beating, after Bible readings they still got them. There was no forgiveness, and our punishment was always brutally physical.

We were so scared of the duppy, and we read the Bible because we were afraid the obeah man was right.

Sometimes at night at the neighbor's house I was dying to sleep but was too scared to go to my yard for fear I might run into the duppy. I would wait for Paula and Julie until they were ready to sleep as well. We were all so scared of the duppy that we would make a dash for our yard together. Around the corner we would come running from Sonita and Trevor's house up the steps to our house, running from a duppy we had never seen or heard. It was very nerve-racking when my mother would lock the door. We were in the pitch black of night waiting for her to let us in. When she took too long we feared that the duppy man or woman might get us.

Sometimes because she did not open the door on time and the fear would set in after waiting too long, we would race back to the neighbor's house. The blessed neighbors, Sonita and Trevor, a young married couple, always let us back in their little room, even if they were tired and wanted to go to bed. It was almost as if they were expecting us to run back. They were just as terrified of the ghosts as we were.

In the mornings when the beatings were over, the scriptures were read, and I took out the chimmy and washed it and placed it under the bed for the night, my day could begin. I got ready for school. Julie and Paula went to public school, but I went to a private school where my mother was a maid.

Mother was lucky in landing a domestic job at St. Cecelia Preparatory School, one of the most elite, prominent, and sophisticated schools in the country. I was lucky to be in the right place at the right time when she could no longer find a sitter for me and I ended up going to work with her every day.

I was instructed to stay in the back in the maid's quarters with the other auxiliary workers while my mother cleaned the house or cooked lunch for the boarders and students when Cookie the cook was off.

Mother worked in the laundry area sometimes and even cleaned classrooms. It was difficult for them to keep me in the back when I was so curious about learning and so much more was happening in the front.

I had never seen so many Anglo-Saxons in one place in my life. I did not know that there were any white facilities still left in my county after slavery. I had listened to stories my grandmother told me about blacks and slavery and the rich white folks.

After seeing so many white children in one

place, I wanted to go to school and be with them. Every day I would stand outside their classroom window looking in. I was learning and wanted to be a part of that. *If only they would only give me a chance,* I thought.

I started to raise my hand at the questions the teacher was asking from outside the classroom window if I knew the answer. One day a teacher named Miss Cameron invited me into her classroom and gave me a seat. It was a big mistake, because I never left. Every day I went to class whether she invited me in or not; I went in and took my seat. I was so thrilled I was going to school again.

I was very fortunate to be given a second-hand uniform and an exercise book my mother cut in half so it would last me longer. As soon as the books were filled up, I would erase their contents and pretend they were like new.

Mother could not afford to buy me a new exercise book when I needed one, so it was a highlight of my life when she stopped cutting them in half. It made me feel like I was finally equal to my peers.

I was so happy when the school took me in, because it meant I would attend and that I would have a shot at a good life. I became the envy of my siblings, who never forgave me.

I was beaten, mocked, and jeered at by my siblings for having white friends. I had acquired friends who lived in the wealthiest neighborhoods in Jamaica—Beverly Hills, Stony Hills, and Jacks Hill—and was getting invited to their lavish birthday parties with limousine service. My siblings could not live with that.

It was hell creating balance as a child. When I went home I had no friends, because the children in my neighborhood did not know me. I did not attend the same school as my siblings and their friends who went to the school in our community.

I always felt like an outcast and a stranger outside my school and inside my home. My siblings taunted me at home every waking hour. They would tell me my mother sent only me to a good school and not them. They were mean-spirited and selfish sisters and made me suffer. In their hearts they knew the circumstances of how I ended up attending St. Cecelia Preparatory and that Mother could never afford such an education otherwise. They believed that if they could not attend the school then neither should I.

Mother started to hate the pressure of her job. She did not want me to play with the other children at my school. How was I to survive with no friends at school and no friends at home and my envious siblings giving me grief?

I was no longer allowed to play with my best friend Natalie Cole, because my mother claimed that the obeah man said that Natalie gave me obeah candy to harm me. My poor friend did not understand that I had become distant from her because I was afraid of what would happen to me at home if I was caught playing with her.

Over the years I was invited to my friends' lavish birthday parties. I could never afford to bring a gift, but I received many gifts only to have them broken by my sister Julie as soon as I arrived home.

When we were kids we didn't have toys except for the ones we made. Aunt Ivy on my father's side of the family lived in England and sent my father's mother, "Grandma Lucy," a barrel filled with things at least once a year. One year a scarecrow effigy came in the barrel for Julie. That was the first thing she ever owned that was closest to a doll.

I had never seen a doll in our house till then. Jules refused to share her scarecrow with me, so that same week, my mother had took me to the market and bought me a doll for a dollar for the first time.

I was almost ten years old. My doll was beautiful to me. I loved it and took special care of it, and everyone noticed that.

Out of the blue one day my sister Julie came out while I was playing with my doll in a quiet and safe place with her scarecrow, a very strong scarecrow, and said, "Let's fight!" meaning her scarecrow and my fragile doll.

She held up her scarecrow. While I tried to shield my doll from her scarecrow's blows, she broke my doll to pieces. She was happy and proud that she had destroyed my doll, and no amount of tape and glue could put it back together. It was thrown out to make peace.

Within the same year my principal gave my mother some stuff including a walky-talky doll; only it could not walk nor talk. Although it was broken, it was perfect to me. It had nice hair, which I loved to comb. We were not allowed to play with the doll my mother had named Marlene. We always knew that Mother kept stuff that she did not want us to get into, along with the opened condensed milk, in that suitcase high on top of the wardrobe.

When my family was all out of the house, I would climb on a chair to reach that doll, and I would play with it from inside the suitcase. It was then that I came across the milk that was hidden, so I would also take a sip from the can. It was a pity that I did not know that the lumps in the milk were not lumps.

One day I came down from the chair to check what was in my mouth. They would not melt, and the lumps had a funny taste. To my horror, they were not lumps in my mouth but cockroaches from the milk.

The worst part was that I could not tell my mother or my siblings that there were roaches in the milk. If I did, Mom would know I was in the suitcase playing with her doll. How else would I have found the roachy milk? I could not tell because I knew the murderation I would get, so I decided to be silent on the issue.

I drank my tea black the next morning, pretending I did not know they were having the roachy milk. I simply could not tell on myself out of fear of being beaten.

All this time Mother and Mr. Barnold continued to date and practice their obeah each day. My mother was using up all her resources on obeah because of this man, and we were suffering as a result.

I had the biggest toothache in the world. My mother could not afford to send me to a dentist, and Mr. Barnold was tired of listening to my complaints. Everyone was tired of my screams and the banging of my head on the board house night and day. My dental appointment at the free clinic was two months away and I could not bear the pain.

Mr. Barnold decided that he had heard enough of my complaining. Instead of loaning my mother the money so I could go to a dentist, he got a pair of pliers from his toolbox in his truck and hid them behind his back.

He called me and told me to open my mouth and show him the cavity that was hurting me. As soon as he spotted it, unbeknownst to me, with the pliers in his giant hands, he reached into my mouth and latched onto my tooth.

I had no time to react, and without any anesthetic or mercy he pulled my tooth so that he would not have to hear again how much I was suffering.

Mother could not see that he was not good for us. He was a middle-class citizen, and we were getting poorer going from one obeah man to the next as fast as he referred her to them.

She did not realize that we were being left behind because she could not afford to buy us anything. Instead she sacrificed our innocence for a piece of land so she could plant peas on his abandoned property and get free mangoes to supplement our diet. There was no money left after all she paid to the obeah men Mr. Barnold introduced her to.

Sometimes Mr. Barnold gave her a loan for paying the obeahman. We had to help her repay him by working in his field planting peas and corn or whatever he said. Sometimes he would take us in his truck and leave us there all day to work under the boiling sun with no food or drink. At the end of the day Mother was sometimes lucky and he let her have a cup of dried beans from the bags we had gathered.

I always hated when Mother would send us to the garden with him alone. I would run away and hide in the bushes for fear of his sick eyes upon me. I was not surprised when my sister was caught stealing. Mother had sent her to live with him and his wife and family. Their world was shaken when my fourteen-year-old sister became pregnant by this man, but I was not surprised. How could Mother not have known? What man takes little girls to lonely beaches?

On several occasions Julie begged Mom to let her come home. She promised Mom that she would be good, but Mother refused to give Julie a chance or allow her to return home. Julie tried to tell Mother what this man was doing, but Mother refused to hear it and accused Julie of making up stories. Mother said that this man was good to keep her and look after her with his children, all of whom were much older men as well.

This man told Mother that Julie was doing well in his home and was a good housekeeper for his wife. He said that his wife was teaching my sister how to be a good homemaker. Julie was allowed to go to school but was no longer allowed to come home.

I soon turned twelve and we moved to Verbena Avenue. The day Julie came home looking pregnant; Mother took her to see Dr. Right, whom she worked for on Saturdays. My fourteen-year-old sister was indeed pregnant by this man. Mother was so upset that she knocked Julie off the chair in the doctor's office after the results came back positive. Julie could have lost the baby she was carrying my niece Camilla. The doctor and the staff had to restrain Mother. After that revelation and that episode, Julie was allowed to come home for good.

Mother finally learned her lesson and realized that all these years we had been telling her the truth about Mr. Barnold. It took a baby to open her eyes to this pedophile. Julie did not need to explain anything to me, because as soon as I saw her I knew. I was just lucky it was not me and I had escaped. Within a few months Julie gave birth to Camilla.

Mother could not stand the disgrace and soon decided she would run away from her problems again. She hated her job and told me that as soon as I reached high school she would quit.

That same year, I passed the common entrance exams and would be the first in my family to attend a high school. No one was excited for me because it meant money for school supplies, books, and a uniform for me. Mother was happy that she did not have to go back to work at my school. I was worried that I would not be able to go to high school because no one cared about me. They were all looking out for themselves.

Mom had a little shop at the front of the yard. She could barely keep it afloat because she credited practically everything to the gunmen who came to buy from her. She did so out of fear and for protection for us, especially during election time.

The gunmen assumed that we were in the same political party as they were because my mother had been so good to them. They forced out a neighbor in our yard who did not belong to their party. They had taken over our yard and branded us as belonging to their party JLP (Jamaica Labor Party).

My mother was neither JLP nor PNP (People's National Party). She was not accustomed to voting and did not allow us to discuss politics, especially in our home. That was forbidden. We decided to go along with them and pretended that Mother was a member of their party to keep our family safe until the election wars ceased so we could get a chance to move out.

We ended up needing protection because the other party took shots at our house, saying we were harboring their enemies. Pity they did not know that we belonged to neither party and would harbor anyone who could guarantee our safety until we could climb to safer ground.

Our house was surrounded by gunmen day and night. Even on the roof men were sleeping with guns to protect us. We were scared inside and outside the house, day and night.

One night when they came to shoot our house I was hiding in the kitchen cupboard. I was on the top shelf. I was so close that I could hear the machine guns cranking up when they came to kill us. Everyone was hiding in a spot he or she had previously picked out.

As the gunshots blazed, I started to relieve my bladder onto my mother, who was hiding under the bottom shelf. I am still convinced that God saved us, because from not even a foot away I am not sure how they did not hear the water running through the cupboard.

Throughout the election, with bullet holes

in the walls of the house, we fretted about when they would return. Many of our neighbors were gunned down in cold blood. What would start like a normal day outside playing with the neighbor's children would soon turn into gunshots and everyone heading for cover.

Sometimes when the shots started to break out we would dive to the ground on our stomachs and shuffle to the house. The last one in would reach up and lock the door. We would then huddle together and listen to them outside.

We prayed every time that the killers would not shoot at our door with their high-powered guns. We stopped sleeping in our beds out of fear. My brother Owen said he would not sleep under his bed; he would rather die in his bed if he must.

Election time is one of the most difficult and violent times in Jamaica for finding a place to rent. Mother had become desperate again and looked to Mr. Barnold again for help, in spite of what had happened to Julie.

We needed to get out of Verbena Avenue fast because the violence in the area and threats were more than we could take. The men protecting our house started to die from frequent attacks from the opposing party. Mother had to close her shop. The monies owed to her were never collected.

My brother Rock came to live with us for the first time during those hard times. He was nearly thirty years old, and it was the second time I had cast my eyes on him since I was a child. The stress level in the house was already high because of the violence and lack of money.

Julie hated him with a passion and would not let him be, but Rock was also not lucky with the family who abandoned him all these years. He came into our home and our lives and tried to fit in, but he was never given a fair chance by my mother or my siblings.

One day Rock smacked Camilla on her hands for playing with matches. Julie became very enraged. She swore at Rock as he tried to explain himself. Julie pulled a machete and a knife and threatened Rock that she would kill him. She picked up Camilla and went after my brother.

I ran away because I did not want to watch what was about to happen. I ran to tell my mother, who was in the front of the yard, what was taking place in the kitchen. By the time Mother and I returned to the kitchen, Julie was running with Camilla and a knife in one hand and a machete in the other. She fell on the knife in front of me and Mother after being hit on the head with a bottle by Rock, who was defending himself from her attacking him.

My mother and sisters did not forgive him.

They threw him out of the house even though they knew he had no money and nowhere to go and had just defended himself because Julie attacked him.

The violence and crime were deadly in Kingston at this time. Even my brother Owen, who always came home very late at night, had started to come home before sundown because he did not want to get captured and decapitated.

It was a time when men who went missing always turned up dead. It was as if that was what they wanted for Rock when they turned him out to the bullets and mercy of the world.

Camilla is now single and has given her own two children much more than a smack on their hands. But it has been more than thirty years, and my family still has not forgiven Rock for saving his own life from Julie that day.

Mother decided to take Mr. Barnold's offer to rent a room from him, as the danger had increased for us at Verbena Avenue because of politics and we could not find anywhere else to live. We moved into a huge empty house owned by Mr. Barnold on Waltham Park Road. With Rock gone, all eight of us were put in one room while the rest of the house, though empty, was locked off to us.

The room was not big enough to hold all of our belongings, so Mother was forced to store almost everything we owned in the garage. We did not own a vehicle. Mother was forced to put our books in the cupboard in the garage.

I was the only one going to school at that time and the only one using the books in the cupboard as a bookshelf. Mother had kept her money from the shop she had to close in a jar hidden in the bookshelf without anyone's knowledge and had forgotten. Although I was the only one using the bookshelf, I had not seen the money in the jar.

Mother searched for the money for months. She was sure that she had misplaced it during the move. Every day we searched for the jar of money. We searched the room and the garbage over and over again. The stress of not finding the money took a toll on all of us.

One day when I came home from school Mother was very unhappy with me. She claimed that she remembered hiding the money in the cupboard with the books I was using and that I had to have known what happened to the money.

I was shocked that she would accuse me of such a crime. I tried to explain that I did not find or keep her money. She did not believe me, and I had no way of convincing her that I did not know the money was hidden behind the books I was using every day.

It was the first time I was ever accused of

stealing, and I did not know how to handle the situation. Mother decided that the money in the missing jar would have been enough for my lunch money and bus fare to school for about a year, so I should use that money she believed I had found for school. I did not find the money that she accused me of finding. What was I to do?

The only way I could get to school was to walk from Molynes Road and Waltham Park Road where I lived to Meadowbrook High School up Red Hills Road. It is a very lonely area to be walking alone with rumors of the fable of the black-heart man going around again. As a child we were threatened to never run away from home because the black-heart man would kidnap us. He is the one who stores up the hearts of little children.

I had to walk to school in this area where girls often went missing when I was still haunted and had a fear of the unknown. Then, after a long, exhausting, and fearful journey to school, I arrived hungry and thirsty with no lunch money. At lunchtime I tried not to lose my friends, who always shared with me because I was honest with them. They knew the situation that I was in at home.

God bless Mr. Pecker, selling in his little cart his nutritious calaloo (a green leafy vegetable similar to spinach), bread or ackee (Jamaican national fruit, never eaten unless it opens on its own), and salt fish and bread. He would even credit you with a bag of sky juice until you could afford to pay him if you were hungry and thirsty.

I was blessed with great friends throughout my life that supported me when I needed them. Sometimes my friends would pool their bus fares so I could eat lunch. We would then walk home after school. If I were super lucky we would take the bus together if someone had extra money to pay my fare. Those were the most loyal friends anyone could have.

Meanwhile I had stopped studying at home in the garage for fear of Mother losing something else there. Six months later Paula decided to move in with a policeman with a restaurant. I got lucky, because for the next few months she let me come once a week for ten dollars, which she claimed she stole from the till.

She never had money that was clean to help anyone, because what she made she kept strictly for herself. I could not complain about where it came from, because now my suffering had ceased a bit. The ten dollars was enough for bus fare to go to school, and I could eat lunch anytime I decided to walk.

One day after I got home Mother presented me with the empty money jar. It had been almost a year. She said Julie gave her the jar and told her that she had found it in my bookshelf. Finally my mother believed me. Mother told Julie that she had been in my bookshelf over and over and the money jar was not there and that the empty jar could not have just appeared.

She had just realized that Julie had been taking us all for a ride while I was suffering. She realized that I was innocent and was being treated like I was guilty. What good was an apology to me anyway if I were to get one when my words and my feelings had been ignored?

For months I was treated like a thieving liar when I had been telling the truth. Julie would never be able to take back the hurt she had caused me during my studies. All this time Julie watched me suffered going to school and supported Mother. She did not know that Julie had taken the money and that I was innocent. In my heart I cried every waking day over my innocence.

I thought maybe Mother spent the money and had forgotten during the packing and the moving. Everyone in the house had taken turns to look for it including Julie, the culprit, and the money was still nowhere to be found. One of the hardest things to prove is your innocence when everyone thinks you are guilty.

After they realized I was innocent they would not tell me they were sorry. That meant they'd have to accept that they were wrong and had caused me great suffering.

The next day my life returned to normal, and after nearly one year I started to receive lunch money and bus fare for school again. I was happy that the truth came out and I was able to return some kindness to my friends when they needed me.

I hoped this would never happen to me again when I would be judged guilty despite being innocent. If only mother would also agree to pay my school fees now and buy the books I needed for school, but that was just a dream. I longed for the day when I would not have to hide from the principal who came to check and throw students out of class if their fees were not paid.

Despite all that was spent on obeah, we seemed to be suffering more, and even though we slept in the same bed at nights, instead of growing closer, the distance between us grew wider than ever. Wherever we moved to live, the duppies seemed to find us. There was never enough money to keep them away.

Julie was fifteen and still could not read or write. She had to drop out of school to have the baby. She was envious of me because I was still going to school, even though I took care of my niece Camilla in the evenings so she could go to JAMAL (Jamaica Movement for the Advancement of Adult Literacy). I also helped her with her homework, though she repaid me with evil behind my back.

When everyone else told her how useless she was and tore her down, I built her courage and helped her up. Nothing they could do to me could break me any further. All I could think about was family and how I could build them up. It is amazing how they took the greatest pleasure in hurting me whenever they could, and I could never return the favor.

Joining the JCCF (the Jamaica Combined Cadet Force) with my friends was the best thing I ever did for myself at that age. It gave me discipline, stamina, determination, patience, understanding, and whatever I needed to be able to survive the backstabbing and the infighting. Staying in school was my uppermost priority, because it promised me the hope of what I could become: a gift only I could give myself.

Mr. Barnold denied being the father of Julie's baby and did not want to accept responsibility. It was too shameful of a situation to be in, since Mr. Barnold had come to the aid of my mother and then impregnated my fourteen-year-old sister. He tried to pass it off on his four sons, but they were insulted by their father's accusations. Everyone knew that the truth was staring at them, because the baby looked exactly like him. He was outraged and demanded that we move out of his house, now!

Mother was in a situation again. Elections were over. JLP (Jamaica Labor Party) won; PNP (People's National Party) lost. The violence had calmed down in most areas, and it was safe to move again during this time.

Mother found a place in Cross Roads on Retirement Crescent close to John Mills All Age School where she became a higgler at the school gate along with a few other women. The house was like a mansion of old Victorian character and may have been built in the 1800s and abandoned by wealthy white folks.

We call it "Ratter Castle," because it was rat infested. The rats, some almost as big as cats, lived in the house and in the old abandoned rotten scrapped vehicles all over the property. Whenever you entered the kitchen, there was a rat jumping from the counter and dashing for a hole.

It looked like an old haunted house with busted windows dangling from the attic high above. From the roadside it was hard to tell if the house was red or grey because it was so old, in dire need of repair, and could use a coat of paint. It housed five families.

We were lucky enough to get one bedroom and hall, which I shared with the seven of them; my brother Owen had his room in the hall. There was no water in the pipes in the house, and there was no electricity except for the thieving light they ran under the cellar.

The house was an eyesore of the community. When it rained there was nowhere to sleep because we had to lay out the pots and pans to collect the rain from the leaky roof. It was a disgrace to live there. It was very dilapidated and seemed to have no owner.

We were lucky to live there, but we were also ashamed to give anyone that address. It was so bad that when I was walking down the street if a stranger was walking along with me, I would pass my house and pretend I did not live at that address. When no one was in view I would make a dash up the walkway. It was one step away from living under a bus stop, Mother told us.

Mother met Miss Pee, who had eight children and lived in the room next to ours. Her eldest daughter, Maxin, was my age. We became the best of friends. Miss Pee had to move to Montego Bay, where she had acquired a job in the tourist industry.

Mother had offered to keep Maxin for her until she graduated in a few more years. Miss

Pee would send my mother money as part of the agreement. You could tell when there was no money by the way Mother treated Maxin.

The poor girl was treated worse than us. Mother was very hard on her. She gave her the most difficult chores to complete and insisted that she earn her keep. If she refused or could not complete her task, Mother would not give her a break but insisted that she pay her way or go home to her mother. The poor girl had nothing but was determined to graduate so she could go to secondary school. That's why she opted to stay with us.

Mother would share her food with anger and slide her plate toward her on the counter. I was very sorry for Maxin and wished Mother would direct her energy at me instead of this poor girl. It only lasted a few months before Maxin was broken and could not take the treatment or the beatings any longer.

Mother decided she did not want Maxin

to stay with us anymore because she was too lazy. It became a mutual agreement between the two that Maxin would rather go home without the diploma she wanted so much than continue to live with us. Maxin could not handle it, yet that was how we lived with the beatings all our lives.

The once bright and cheery girl who loved to sing and who sang like a bird became sad, depressed, and withdrawn in a few months. I was happy that she was going home even though she was my best friend and I knew I would never see her again. I knew she was not able to handle the beatings like we were. It broke my heart to see her so unhappy.

Through the darkness there was some light. I had just turned thirteen and Mother had acquired our first black-and-white television set. We were able to watch Lady Diana's wedding to Prince Charles on July 29, 1981.

It was a remarkable occasion viewed for the first time on our own television set.

Though Mother had quit her job at St. Cecelia Preparatory, she kept in contact with Miss Delcie, the ironing lady who still worked there. One day my mother decided to go and visit this lady in her home.

Julie tagged along with her and brought her baby Camilla. Miss Delcie lived on Queen Street in the heart of Kingston in an area with a staggering crime rate. She lived in a tenement yard in a very small room she divided in two to the very back of the yard.

The lady who lived at the front of the yard had two dogs. One was a very mean and vicious dog. That day when they went to visit Miss Delcie the dog was, as usual, very angry at any stranger who came on his territory. It broke down its rotten cage and attacked them while they were passing the cage to go to Miss Delcie's room.

Julie was severely bitten before the owner could contain her dog. She arrived home with bandages on her feet. I felt very sorry for Julie and her experience with the dog.

I later learned that the reason for their visit was to go and see the new place where I would be living. I was shocked at their conspiracy. I could not believe that Mother was sending me to live where that dangerous dog lived. I prayed and begged Mother to not give me away.

My sisters considered that it was only fair if I went through the same hardship that they had endured. I promised Mother that I would do anything for her not to send me away. I cried to my sisters for their help, but they were all in on it. Julie was ecstatic and bursting with joy; she could not wait to see me go. She said it was my turn now that she was able to return home with her baby.

I cried in vain, but my words went in one

ear and out the other. No one helped me. They had been through so much that they had become cold and heartless and made sure I would not escape any of it.

I had no control over anything that was happening to me. I was always fearful of them hurting me because I never learned how to be aggressive, envious, jealous, or mean-spirited like they were. I was always crying and very unhappy in my family. I felt like a misfit and longed to belong.

It was a shock. I had one week to pack my bags. That I was moving to the yard with the dogs was all I could think about. There was no one to help me, and my heart was full of hurt.

I arrived on a Sunday evening with my school bag and a brown shopping bag of clothes that was my suitcase. We knocked at the high gate for about an hour and decided to leave before the woman who owned the dogs came out to see what we wanted and to let us into the yard.

The dogs were barking furiously in their cages. It is no wonder that it was impossible for any knocking to be heard at the gate with all that commotion in the cages. One cage shook violently and was evidently not strong enough to contain the dog for long.

Mother and I quickly scurried by, as Miss Delcie's rooms were way in the back. Miss Delcie was happy to see me, and I pretended that I was happy to see her as well. I was even happier to see that she had a television set. I told myself that if I could get past that dog each day I would be okay. I knew I had no other option but to accept the unacceptable and make the best out of this experience.

Miss Delcie rented two adjoining rooms. She had one bed, which we shared. She also had a refrigerator, which was a luxury to me, seeing that in our home we were never able to afford one. Mother dropped me off once again, this time with a set of rules.

One rule was that I should not try to come home and that I should be grateful that I was being kept for free. I was allowed to come home once a month for lunch money and bus fare to school, but it was never enough money. I was allowed only one meal per day.

I was given two fishes and one cabbage per week to prepare for my supper after school. Miss Delcie was poor herself and ate her supper at work before she came home so she could save her money.

After the first week the neighbors complained that I was wasting electricity watching television, so I was no longer to watch it unless Miss Delcie was home. Nor was I allowed to use power at night to study, so I was given a kerosene lamp.

I was so sad at night that even when I did not want to study I did not want to crawl into bed with her. She was not my family. I wanted to go home to my family where I belonged.

At Miss Delcie's, I was not free to come and go. It was like living in prison with a vicious dog guarding the entrance. Even when taking a shower I had to plan how I would make a dash without the dogs seeing me.

There was always a surprise waiting for me in the shower. The croaking lizards, some as long as my arm, lived in the rotten boards in the ceiling. They came out to take baths and drink water from time to time; they were always there to greet me. I was terrified of the eyes watching me shower. I was fearful and on guard that the lizards would rush me.

The neighbor was always yelling at me to shake my clothes out in the shower before I put them on. After hanging on the door the lizards or scorpions might have gotten into them, and I could be severely bitten.

Miss Brown was Miss Delcie's closest

neighbor and friend. Sometimes she would give me some of her supper so I would get a break from the fish or the cabbage. One day Miss Brown gave a bowl of stew beef with gungo pea soup. It was very tasty and delicious. I was very hungry and enjoyed the soup. Then, for a moment I took a pause and really looked into my soup. I saw what appeared to be little white maggots: dead and floating, their little black eyes staring up at me. I wanted to be sure so I opened a pea, and there was a worm inside. I panicked.

I was no longer hungry and felt ill. I needed to dispose of the rest of the soup without drawing attention to myself and disturbing everyone else. I found a crack in the wooden floor through which I poured the rest of the soup.

I was shocked to hear the dogs racing to get the hot soup I was pouring under the cellar. I could hear everyone outside wondering what in God's name the dogs were racing for, but I kept silent and waited for a convenient time to return the bowl. I thanked her for the meal.

When I did get in the yard, I left in the mornings when Miss Delcie left for work. That way, I was able to safely pass the dogs with her. In the evenings after school when I returned I would sometime knock and wait for hours at the gate, but no one came to let me in. I would sooner give up and return to the bus stop where I waited for my friend who had a friend with a bus.

I would travel with my friends into the high dangerous hills, with deep precipices far below us. I was scared to look out the bus window, especially at night. I went home whenever I could get in, and if I could not get in, I would ride on the bus all night and sometimes all day trying to check home from time to time.

Sometimes I would not be able to get in the yard for days because no one would answer but the dogs. I went to school every day, but after school I waited with my friend so we could pass time riding on the bus if I could not get in at home. I became homeless at age fourteen and was living on the street. My family did not want me anymore, and it was my turn to be abandoned and hardened.

It was as if it was a "rite of passage" and it was my turn, according to my siblings. Many nights when I could not go home before I fell asleep on the bus I would think about them. I wondered if they even remembered or missed me.

I wondered about Mother and if her heart ached at nights when she thought of me, or did she cry at nights when I did not come home? Did her heart break to give me away, or did she just feel relieved and thank God I was gone?

I often wondered whether she thought of me like I thought of her. I was not surprised;

nor did I wonder, “Why me?” I always knew that it was just a matter of time before it would be my turn and I would be pawned away like a kitten in the litter like Rock and the others.

To me it was all about survival when I was on my own. I knew once I got to school I would be all right until school was dismissed at three o’clock.

As for taking a shower, the YMCA on Hope Road was always a blessing, because I was always welcome to a shower and a swim. It was a really great and positive environment for me in my situation and became my favorite place to pass the time. I had decided, along with six of my friends at school—Marcia, Aleith, Rosemarie, Prudence, Unas, and Maureen—to join the army cadets to kill more time.

We were not even in third form but were all suffering in high school. We needed a way out of the financial hardship. Unas was homeless for political reasons, and I was practically homeless because where I lived a dog kept me out and my own family had no use for me. They would not allow me to come home no matter how I begged them.

We could not go to our friends' houses because their parents were also poverty stricken and could not afford to take us in. Even under normal circumstances we were not to visit, much less move in; that would be out of the question.

If we did visit, we had to pretend we stopped by to drop off homework or came for a drink of water, which was when we would be allowed to visit. My own mother also did not welcome my friends into her home.

I came up with a plan to join all the extracurricular activities that I could join for free so that all my waking hours would be filled up. I joined dancing, netball, softball, hockey, and drama for extra classes. Those activities gave me a place to belong and the opportunity to stay out many hours in the evenings until late. On the other days I would stay at the YMCA learning how to swim.

At nights after everything was over, I would try to go home to Miss Delcie's. If she heard me calling, I was in. If she did not hear me calling and knocking, I would have to go and spend the rest of the night riding on my friends' bus if they were on it. If they were not, I waited at the bus stop till five in the morning for the first bus to arrive to go to school.

Sometimes I was the first student to arrive at school. The school and classrooms were in darkness. I would turn on the lights in my classroom building as if it was my home. I was always happy to see the next student to arrive.

Living at Miss Delcie's lasted nearly two years. I begged my family to take me back, but they refused to. Mother made it pretty clear to me I should stay where I was living because she was finally retired and moving back to the country.

I needed her help to make it through school, but once again she let me down. The ratter castle they lived in was falling apart, and the men at Joel Gibbs' studio next door started to complain that the house was giving the studio bad luck and making it bad for their business. They threatened to burn it down as soon as my family and the rest of the squatters moved out.

Mother promised me that as soon as my sisters got a place to rent they would take me back. By the time I reached third form I was allowed to return home. They found a two-bedroom duplex house to rent. I was fifteen years old, and for the first time in my life I had my own single bed.

I shared a room with the four of them: Madonna and her daughter, Nadinola, on one bed, and Julie and her daughter, Camilla, on the bed across from my panel-folding bed with the kaya (made from dried coconut bark) mattress. It was like sleeping on a bed of pins, but I was grateful because it allowed me a place to sleep with a roof over my head and not at the bus stop with all the mentally ill, intoxicated, or homeless people.

I went to school every day even if I had to go on foot. Not going to school meant that I would jeopardize my future. I knew I was in a good high school and that once I was in I had to stay or I would lose my place.

I worked hard at trying to keep up with the rest of the students even without the books. My sisters would not buy the books or supplies I needed even though they had jobs.

My brother Owen, who only came home once in a while, tried to help me out as much as he could. Whenever he could he would give me bus fare and lunch money for school and buy me one or two of the textbooks. It was such pressure picking only two when all the books were important. The librarian became my best friend and savior and was lenient to me and did not make me pay all my fines.

I would still often walk to school and eat no lunch because I was saving to pay for something I needed for school. My friends and I were in the same predicament financially. We stuck together for the five years of high school and were always there for each other. Marcia's father had passed away when she was a baby, and she was raised by her evil grandmother, who also beat her daily. Her mother was unable to take care of her because she had had too many children and there was no father around.

Marcia's uncle Bobby was somehow in charge of Marcia's financial welfare. He worked at the wharf down by the seaside. We needed to take two buses to get to his workplace so she could get money for school.

We would take the bus from school to go downtown and walk what felt like nearly ten miles in the hot sun to his workplace. Sometimes he would not come out to see us, knowing that we were coming and how far we had come. Sometimes he would send a message from security after we'd already waited there roasting in the hot sun for hours behind the fence "come back tomorrow." Poor Marcia's heart would be broken, and she would cry. We would all cry along with her.

Sometimes we had no money and had to walk all the way home. We would not arrive home until dark only to meet at school to plan when we would go back again. Sometimes it was weeks before we could plan the trip again, and she would also have to do without.

Unfortunately for some of us and for me especially, there was no one to pay the school fees. At my house no one cared whether I attended school or not. It was up to me to fight to stay in school.

The principal of Meadowbrook High School, "Spanna" as she was called because of her fluency in Spanish(Mrs.McLennon), was always looking and chasing students out of the classrooms if their school fees were not paid. Sometimes she was on a roll for days. We would be unable to relax or stay in class, because as soon as we heard "Spanna is coming" the entire class would be disrupted as unpaid students dispersed.

Even though it was such a shameful situation, I took comfort in knowing that I was not the only one. My friends and I became accustomed to walking home together almost every evening from school to save money.

We would especially enjoy the walk during mango season because along the way we had the opportunity to gather all different types of mangoes, namely East Indian mangoes, black mangoes, Bombay mangoes, and Julie mangoes. It was the only time of the year when we could afford to bring anything home for our families.

I had a little further to walk to get to my house. One day I decided to take a shortcut through Olympic Way and Seaward Drive with my friends Marcia, Maureen, and Rosemarie, who stayed in that area in Olympic Gardens. All of a sudden we walked into a group of men who were firing guns at each other.

We ran away in a panic and frenzy in different directions. Even after ten minutes of running, I could hear shots firing in the direction my friends ran. We had no telephones, so it was impossible to know if they got away alive. The next day at school when we saw each other we realized it was a miracle that none of us had been shot.

School, my friends, and my extracurricular activities were the most exciting things going on in my life as a teenager. I took particular interest in cadets, as that had given me the discipline, skills, and endurance needed to overcome what I was up against in my family. It had prepared me for my journey through life.

When I turned sixteen years old I met and fell in love with Hubert, a guy four years my senior. I thought he would be my first and last love. I used to see him strolling by my house every evening with his brother and his friend. As time went by we became friends and started to go to the movies together. When I decided to introduce Madonna and Julie to him and his friends, it turned out to be the biggest mistake of my life.

To my surprise Madonna started to date his friend, although he was much younger than she was, and Julie started to date my boyfriend's brother. I was very upset and embarrassed about their relationships with my friends, especially because I was not comfortable with two sisters going with two brothers.

I made it pretty clear to everyone that I was not comfortable in this scenario. Madonna decided that now that I had a boyfriend he should feed me and send me to school and give me everything I needed to survive. My boyfriend was barely twenty years old and still lived with his parents. They were wardens in the penitentiary and treated their children as if they were hardcore criminals, beating them with whips and batons. We were not allowed to go to his house.

One Sunday evening I had gone to the Odeon Theatre in Half-Way Tree with my boyfriend. After the show, which ended around 11:00 p.m., he decided to walk me home first before he went home. As we got inside my gate, men appeared out of nowhere firing gunshots and running up and down the road.

We made it to the veranda just two feet

from the door and window to our house. I saw my sister Madonna come to the window and look directly at us crouched behind the small veranda column that was sheltering us from the bullets.

We raced over to the door, thinking she was going to let us in. I was shocked when she closed the curtain and left us outside in the bullets. Since she did not open the door, we had to run back to our hiding place behind the column.

After the shots ceased, we decided to brave the streets and go back to the Half-Way Tree Park (now called Nelson Mandella Park) to spend the night. It was not safe to stay there all night, and evidently none of my sisters—Julie, Paula, or Madonna—would open the door and let me in. Owen was not home.

We were so cold in the dewy night in the park. I could tell that Hubert wanted to go home, because unlike me he was not used to sleeping outdoors. He later ended up losing his best friend, who chose Madonna over him.

Madonna had stopped giving me food to eat, and I was not allowed to use the pots and pans. I was also not allowed to use the stove to prepare anything to eat. I was so desperate that I concocted what I liked to call the milo tin stove. I used a large empty tin can with a lid. I punched holes about two inches from the rim. Then I filled the holes with wicks made from cloth and poured kerosene oil in the can to soak the wicks. Then I lit all the wicks. I could prepare all my meals by controlling how high I pulled the wick through the holes to control the fire.

The food was cooked filled with soot and sometimes tasted like kerosene oil, but with nothing else to eat I began to acquire a taste for soot and oil. Hubert tried to find a job and could not find one to help me. He turned to stealing and conning anyone he knew in order to help me to continue going to school. His goal was to make sure that I graduated from high school.

He then did the unthinkable out of desperation for me. My graduation was approaching in July of 1984. There was not enough money to write the exams I wanted to write, and there was no money to buy the clothes I needed for the graduation ceremony or the ball. If it were up to me I would have accepted the fact that I could not attend the ceremony, much less the ball. Hubert's heart would not let me accept that when he knew that all my life I had lived to finish school and to be the first to graduate in my family.

One day while I was at school, unbeknownst to me, Hubert got our key from the neighbor's house and let him-self in. He got into Madonna's savings box, the one Jules admitted she had been going in. He then gave me enough money to buy material to take to the dressmaker to make and pay for my dresses. I still needed shoes and taxi fare to get to the ball, and that would cost sixty dollars. The ball was held at the "Casa Monte Hotel." Everyone at school was so excited about the graduation, taking pictures and all. I had to remain silent; because I was not sure I was going to be there. A few days before the ceremony, Hubert gave me a few more dollars for the shoes and the fare, so I was able to attend my graduation ceremony and the ball. I will always be grateful to him. One downfall to all this was when Madonna began accusing me of stealing the money. I tried to explain that I knew nothing about it, but Madonna would not believe me. I was not supposed to make it to my graduation or the ball; yet I did attend. It was supposed to be a happy time for me, but instead I found myself crying every day because I was innocent. I fell into deep depression, as I was no longer in school and my activities were cut severely. I

I was teaching swimming and working as a lifeguard, making a little money. For the first time in my life I was earning just enough for food.

I soon met Troy at the YMCA. He was also a swimming instructor and lifeguard. I thought I was in love again. This time it was more serious, and just a few months after we started dating, I became pregnant, though I did not know it for almost six months. Madonna would spit on the ground whenever she saw me and made sure to tell me that I made her stomach sick because she said I was carrying a young child. My sisters decided to throw me out of the house when they confirmed that I was pregnant. They soon moved to a place where I could no longer find them because it was obvious that I had been with a boy.

I found myself homeless and pregnant and living in an abandoned house without windows like a mad woman. I could not find my family or anyone to help me. I could no longer fit in a bathing suit, so I lost my job.

I started to see Troy's true colors coming out shortly after it was confirmed that I was with child. He came home to stay with me in the abandoned house only late at night, as if he did not want anyone to see him. All day I had nothing to eat except for the almond nuts the blessed neighborhood children, Maryanne and her friends, gathered for me every day. Every night Troy brought home a quarter of bread and a can of Brunswick sardines for our supper. As soon as I ate I would throw up, because my stomach could not digest the bread, and there was nothing else for me to eat. I was sick and needed my family, but they did not want me even if I could find them. I could not find my father, and I cried myself to sleep every night. At nearly seven months pregnant I got very sick and had to go to the hospital. I was given an emergency surgery to remove an abscess. It was the most barbaric procedure I have ever experienced. I was placed in stirrups and strapped down with my big belly. The surgery was performed without anesthetic. I screamed so loud I am sure the entire hospital and Hope Road and surrounding area must have heard me. My only thought was that this could not have been good for the baby. I prayed for the ordeal to be over so I would be well again for when the baby got here.

During my eight months of pregnancy, Troy and I managed to secure a room to rent on Pretoria Road off Maxfield Avenue in a very bad neighborhood. I had no option but to take it so my son would not be born homeless. I moved in with my single-panel bed and few clothes, some pots and pans, and the car rim I had started to use for a cold stove. I was so happy with my own place for the first time that I prayed in my heart and thanked God for his help.

My life started to change, and the people around me treated me with the kindness and respect that I had never received in my own home. I started to see that there was light in the world and that all was not made of darkness after all. I wondered about hope and dared to dream—and did I ever dream!

Life with Troy was not the bed of roses I had dreamed it would be. If fact, he was mean and abusive and never really knew how to love or give love freely. I lived with him for seven horrible years, all the time dreaming about the future I would one day give myself. I prayed secretly that God would come and rescue me, but not just me—me and my son.

The violence grew in Lower Maxfield Avenue where we lived, so it was no longer safe for Troy to come home from work when he was finished working at the YMCA. His mother decided that since she was going to

Philadelphia to live, Troy and I could have her room so that Troy could be with his son.

On September 3, 1988, while my son and I were living with my Troy and his siblings, Hurricane Gilbert hit Jamaica and took half the house with us inside. It was the most horrifying natural disaster I had lived through. When the winds started to rip the house apart, we tried desperately to hold it together with our bare hands. When we could no longer hold the door shut after being thrown back several feet, several times, the roof started to disappear. We decided to run and hide.

Throughout the storm and the raging winds that battered the house and the howling of the sea, I wondered about everyone else and hoped I would see them again. I hid in my room where we had nailed galvanized zinc over the windows in preparation for the storm. I hung on to my son from behind the bed, where I prayed and waited out the storm.

When it was all over there was total destruction all around us. It took months for us to pick up the pieces of our shattered lives. With no work or food in storage, I came to rely on the truck from the YMCA that came through our area from time to time to drop off food and supplies for hurricane victims.

It was like living in hell when I was living with Troy and his family. It was like living on the edge, having day-to-day dealings with so many different characters in that house, with everyone not wanting us there and letting me know that they already didn't have enough for themselves and would not share with me. I had been broken down, beaten down, threatened, and abused already, so I was well seasoned and prepared to deal with just about anything.

I tried to leave several times, but each time I had to go back for my son, because my heart would not let me leave him behind. The last time I decided to leave Troy, I stayed in a women's shelter with my son. After the first two weeks I took a chance and took my son to school. His father went to the school and took him.

I was forced to go back and stay, because I could not leave him without my child. I stayed for as long as I could and prayed for the day when I would escape. Everyday Troy told me I could not leave him or he would find me and hurt me. I prayed that I would escape in a plane where I would be free and safe in the land of opportunities.

Madonna, who was a domestic helper, was sponsored to work in Canada by the people she used to work for in Jamaica. In a few years she met and married Rolans, who had five children from a previous marriage. She treated them like they were less than dirt. A few years later, with the financial help of Rolans, Madonna was able to sponsor my mother, who in turn sponsored my sisters and their children and Owen, my brother. Owen had quickly given up his place and said, "Let all the girls go first." The most painful part of that dream was when I had to make the decision to leave my son behind. I promised my son that I would send for him as soon as I could. He was left behind with his father Troy, who soon ended up giving him away to a couple who we knew, had failed in having their own children.

My heart was broken when I arrived in Canada without my child. To add to the misery, I ended up living with my evil sisters again, who did not care or wish to hear what happened to my son because they all had their children with them. Their way of comforting me when I was hurting for my son was to tell me to go back, when they knew in their hearts that was not an option.

We arrived in Toronto in early November of 1992 and saw snow for the first time in our lives. They were very happy that their dreams had come true, but I was in tears because I had to leave my son behind. They were very upset with Owen's decision to find me and to let me come to Canada in his place, but I went along with it. God bless his soul.

I had just arrived in Canada and nearly became homeless again, because after all these years I still could not agree with them and their madness of using and discarding people as soon as they had no use for them. I was terrified of the winter and knew no one in this country who could take me in. I had nowhere to go and was afraid that I would be sent home if I became homeless here in Canada.

I was just learning how to take the bus and trying to get accustomed to the vehicles driving on the right-hand side of the road instead of on the left like I was accustomed to in Jamaica.

That added to the stress of my life turned upside down, not being able to find my way around in the horrible cold, coming close to my freezing point on several occasions because of underestimating the weather and trying to walk too far.

I did everything I could to make my sisters like me, but it just was not possible. I was forced out of Madonna's home two months after I arrived in Canada, as soon as I got my first job making 120 dollars a month. She had said that her house had become crowded and I was the fittest to go because my child was left behind.

As soon as I got my first job, I found a place to rent for ninety dollars and decided that the thirty dollars would have to feed me for the month. I had to repay every penny paid toward the sponsorship for me to come to Canada on Madonna's repayment plan. Her repayment plan consisted of the money she paid to the Canadian Immigration for sponsorship fees and the money she paid to the doctors in

Jamaica for the medical examinations prior to entering Canada. I knew if I bought a box of chicken back with leg attached and a bag of rice and a box of noodle soup, I would have food for the month, so I announced I would be moving out. Madonna was very happy and could not wait to see me go.

Rolans wanted to help me get a phone in my apartment and help me get settled. Madonna threatened her husband that if he were to help me it would be over between them. The only help he was able to offer me was to give me a few abandoned cups, pots, and pans from their basement that he had used when he was a bachelor before he met my sister. Rolans's hands were tied, and he was only allowed to give me a ride with my belongings out of their home. I was very grateful for his help once again, because I knew deep down that he was a good man and that it was he who enabled my sister to afford having the six of us from Jamaica at the same time.

Luckily I lived and worked downtown in Regina, so I could walk to work, and often my coworkers at the Energy Doctor gave me a ride home. I prayed for bonuses at work, because that was how I made money. I had saved enough money so that within a year I had paid my debt and I was able to approach Canadian Immigration and get on with sponsoring my son. It took two years for me to be reunited with my son.

Rolans was unaware that, shortly after I moved out of their home, on a trip to Jamaica Madonna would have eyes for one of her countrymen. She came back to Canada and left her perfect husband for one who would not be the one she would spend the rest of her life with but was fooled with empty promises that destroyed her life. She soon married Rolans friend and lived with a man who was obsessed with my mother as he was her age.

The place I rented was so shabby that I was shocked to learn that run-down ratter castles were also in Canada and that people actually lived in them. It was warm, and that was all I cared about. I didn't want to risk being homeless again. It came with a single bed and a chair and half of a table nailed to the wall. There was a stove and fridge in my room and a washroom down the hall that I shared with nine other people. I was shocked to learn that not everyone was rich and had a swimming pool or drove a nice car. Reality set in again, and I realized that life here was no bed of roses and was unlike anything I had expected.

I was happy to move out because at Madonna's house I was not allowed to take phone calls from Jamaica. I could not afford to pay for the calls, because I had just arrived and was not working. Not even our own brother

Rock's phone calls were welcomed by them to this very day. Having my own place gave me the freedom to communicate with my son. It always broke my heart to hear my son cry for me on the other end of the telephone millions of miles across the sea, but it gave me some comfort to know he was just a phone call away.

After all these years of separation from my family they did not change their evil ways. In fact they became more vicious and deadly than any poison affecting their own lives and anyone that they touched. Not only were they obsessed with obeah and duppies, but they were also obsessed with money and destroying lives along the way, turning against even their closest friends to make even a few meager dollars by any conniving way they could think of.

One small fender-bender resulted in the end of an incredible awesome friendship and relationship, because my family decided that the friendship was not worth saving when money was involved. That decision shocked everyone involved, but it was easy for everyone to now see the history of why I like to consider myself separate from them because of their mean and selfish ways. I was like a sore in their eyesight whenever I disagreed with any one of them. I yearned for the freedom to be honest with them, but the price of honesty was far more than I could imagine that was to come.

It was like a miracle for me, because the gods must have been listening when at the lowest point in my life, just when I needed it, I was given a job and a place to call my own. I moved into my one-room ratter castle with an open mind and was very proud of myself and the start of my new life in Canada.

I promised myself that I would still be a good daughter, sister, auntie, mother, and friend and not harden my heart toward my family no matter what. I wanted to do what was right under the sun so the blessings of the higher power could flow upon me and my son and everyone that I cared about.

Having to rely on the power of good over evil has been a reward for me that I continue to embrace. All things are attainable through the power of endurance. Nothing good can be attained with evil intentions.

It was plain that the day my family landed in Canada was the day when they felt that they had died and gone to heaven. All the dreams and all the promises they made to help each other went down the drain. My poor brother Rock, who was not lucky enough to come when we were coming, was left behind because they never kept the promise to help my brothers. Owen died waiting for them to help him, and even after his passing they banded together to eliminate his wife Opal so that they would not have to help her.

I was forced by Paula to destroy Opal's number after I came back from his funeral. I was warned that if I kept in contact with her they would be finished with me also, as Opal would now be needing assistance.

I was still seeking their approval and would have done anything to be in a family of my own. They had no good intentions and were blinded by their greed in collecting material possessions.

I felt obligated because it was me Owen had given up his place to come to Canada for, and now he was dead. Looking for their approval and always trying to be perfect around them, I was always afraid to live freely and be myself for fear of abandonment. Yearning for their approval only to have to come to terms with the fact that I would never be like or be liked by them is not such a bad thing.

When Paula's husband Benja started to have numerous affairs on her, it was me whom she confided in. I thought I was a valuable member of the family at last now that she confided in me and came to me for personal advice.

It turned out that I was wrong to confirm to her that her husband was having the affairs. It backfired on me and caused me to lose the already fragile family I had been working so hard to keep. She did not want to hear the truth. She wanted me to find a way to cover up the truth and to tell her that her husband was not cheating.

I could not have lived with telling her a lie when I had the truth before me. Either way I would have been chastised, so I decided that if I must be chastised, let it be for the truth.

I felt that I could not keep up with their jealousy, deceit, and lies after lies, hurting even some of our most precious and most valuable friends. I refused to back down and support any more lies and infidelities, to stop being their victim but to finally stand up for what I believe in.

When Madonna did the unthinkable and crossed the line and had a relation with the husband of, Gunava a prominent woman who helped us when we needed help the most after we landed, I drew the line with her. I felt I could no longer be kicked out of their home for saying what I truly thought about a situation. I wanted them to know that I did not approve of the way they treated people and I was no longer going to put up with it for their approval.

I finally found my voice. I wanted to speak and to be listened to in my family for the first time. They were not going to have that, because my silence was more important when it was not in their favor. Keeping me silent was keeping me down. I had so much to say with no one to listen.

I was tired of the thieving and lies, the

adultery and the fornications. I was tired of the obeah and the duppies in their houses. I was tired of the child molesters and their threats, and I was tired of the threats and the beatings. I was just too tired to watch and to hold everything in.

I prayed for the peace to come. I worked for the good of everyone in my family. I put my trust in my family only to have my life spat on and to be reminded that I was not to be born—I was a mistake. I could not deal with my family's rejection for a long time. I kept on going back, hoping that they would change and love me, only to get more and more rejection, for the acceptance would never come. Mother always told me to forget them and move on with my life.

The shock of my life was when I received a letter in the mail that I was being sued by Paula for her mental and emotional problems, as if I were her cheating spouse.

It was happening to me again. Not Julia stealing Mother's money or Madonna's money and accusing me and them all buying it and finding out the truth later, but it was happening again I was right and was forced to take a wrong.

Madonna, Julia, and Paula needed to believe the worst about me to make me extinct from the family completely, because I could not tolerate their deceptions. They tried everything in the book possible to get me put away on several occasions to teach me a lesson like their kids were taught.

Everyone whom they had a problem with I was to have a problem with also, and I could not promise them that. I could not fit in because I could not just end a relationship with anyone they decided to malign and cheat and I could not play their evil games hurting others; and neither did I want to.

The moment they made it clear to me that

my life with them was officially over; they made a rule that anyone in the family who associated with me and my son would be treated in the same way that I was treated. In the process I lost all my nieces and nephews, who loved me dearly, because they were forced and threatened not to have relations with me or they would also be abandoned.

Camilla tried to break that rule, and Paula kicked her and her two children out of her life because she refused to not have a relationship with me. Mother broke the rule only after Madonna stole her money and kicked her out.

What I could do for me was to help me to move on with my life without them and encourage me to write this book for my own healing. Moving on has been the best thing for me when I finally learned how to do so.

I had to tell someone that they wanted to imprison for the wrong reasons to get a lawyer, and even though the cost was high, once again it was easier to live with the truth than to let an innocent woman go to jail.

The woman won her case and they lost, and I was never forgiven. I could not stand by and see the injustice against anyone else we knew.

I was happy because I could not live with the fact if I were to be a part of a conspiracy to let another person suffer. At this point, I made a conscious decision to sacrifice my life with my family to stand up for what I believed in, no matter what the consequence was. It is over ten years now since my son became ill after we came back from Owen's funeral in Jamaica.

I paid with my life and my innocent sick son who had nothing to do with this, who was also abandoned by my three sisters because I told the truth. They felt that hurting me was not enough, but it would hurt me terribly to hurt and reject my son also. My son, soon after he came home from the hospital, called his aunt Paula to see why she had not come to visit him in the hospital. Her response to him was never to call her again.

The only explanation I had for that was to explain it to my son as the "family sick". Tommy explained to me that my grandmother was estranged from her family and my mother had to obey my grandmother by not speaking to the rest of the family. They never resolved their differences causing us to be born and not having the privilege of meeting our family. That is the reason why we cannot find our family is a trend that Nadinola (Madonna's daughter) and I wanted to break for our children before she contracted the family sickness.

Looking back to there and now with all they put me through I am the woman I was meant to be because my experiences have left me strong and bold and fearless. I am still grateful that throughout all of this I did not lose my identity and I got to be a better me without them. As soon as I started to accept that I had lost them, I could feel the burden starting to lift and my true life starting to come in, and I realized that it was not that bad after all.

I still have the mind to think about them and especially when I hear from my brother Rock in Jamaica, whom I still keep in touch with and help. My other siblings abandoned him as soon as they landed. He is not allowed to have not even their phone numbers to this present day.

Rock went to jail recently, and I needed to post bail so that he could be released as he was innocent. In spite of the fact that my sisters had not spoken to me for years, I tried to see if in the name of family and brotherhood they could find it in their hearts to put our differences aside and to come through for one of our own who was in dire need of our help—what a difference the family would make.

My plea to them landed on deaf ears. It had been almost a decade since they had spoken to me, and they had also forced my mother to stop communicating with me from time to time by tampering with her phone and monitoring her phone calls.

It had been almost a year since Mother and I had to stop communicating as she became unreachable because her phone was not working when I tried to reach her to tell her of Rock's dilemma. I wanted to help him to get bail, because I had spoken to my brother and he was innocent. I called my mother on the telephone. It took several days to reach her to pass on the news to the rest of the family and to let everyone know that I was seeking their help in order to make bail for our brother Rock. My mother's response from her and my sisters was to "let him rot in jail." I was shocked. I could never do that. I thought I had heard wrong. I begged until I was told to leave them alone or else. I was diverted by my mother to Tommy, who tried to hold onto the bail money with his idle hands, and I was laughed at by all of them for trying. I did not give up. If I had stayed closed minded and distrusting and self-absorbed like they were, my brother would more than likely still be in prison, innocent, up to this day.

When I think of what I am able to do without them, I would not have been able to do with them or they would not have allowed me to help out even poor Rock, our own brother. I would not allow them to convince me to abandon my brother Rock like I was made to abandon Owen's wife after he passed away. It was only a few months since Rock lost his adopted father Mass Vintent while he grieved in jail, and no sooner was he out then his adopted mother also passed away.

I tried to contact my mother, whom I had stopped communicating with because Madonna claimed that Mother was wasting money on calling me on the phone, which was not true. I was the only one on this planet who always told my mother, "Hang up and I will call you back."

Mother was sick and left unsupervised and locked up for hours in the bathroom crying and trying to get out. Her phone was cut off from me and everyone she knew. She complained to us that she could not afford to pay for someone to stay with her as she was old and sick.

Mother's phone privileges were cut because Madonna felt that she was telling people things about her lack of care. Mother complained that they were using her money without her permission and that she had become worried about her financial future because of them.

My eighty-seven-year-old mother was recently kicked out of Madonna's house because she continued to complain that they were still using her money on themselves and the guests they had recently sponsored from Jamaica for show instead of helping their only brother and his children left behind in Jamaica who was in dire need of help.

Mother now stays with Nadinola and her six children and is able to connect with the world again. My brother Rock and I are closer than ever, and I would not be happy with it any other way. All of this has made me stronger than I thought I could ever be. I have learned how to count my blessings and to take all my disappointments as a lesson.

Because my wealth cometh from God I am rich enough to be able to forgive them and move on, just as Mother wanted me to do. I set out to accomplish who I am, what I am born to be: a good mother, daughter, sister, and friend. Every day I am excited about the next day now that I am free from their bondage and have the courage to move to the light.

Through the focus of work, prayers, and what is good comes incredible healing of the mind and the soul, and the pieces of the heart can be made whole again. I am now able to make amends with the past and to really embrace the new challenges of life with dignity, pride, confidence, and determination. Through forgiveness, faith, love, and affection comes incredible healing of the heart, mind, and the soul, and the pieces of the past can be laid to rest.

About the Author

Jennifer Lewis is a contractor in Saskatchewan, Canada.

Jennifer Lewis is a fourth-year university anthropology student. She lives in Saskatchewan, Canada, with one cat and a few houseplants. She volunteers for seniors and the disabled. She enjoys writing, and this is her first book.